this journal belongs to

Shreya

Live, Love, Hedgehog.

Follow Your Dreams!

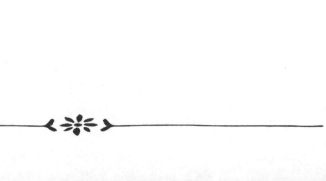

This above all: to thine own self be true.

                                  - Shakespeare

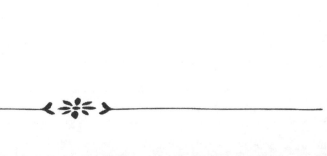

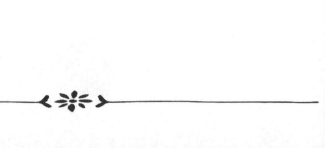

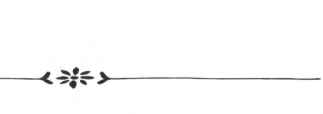

You're looking sharp!

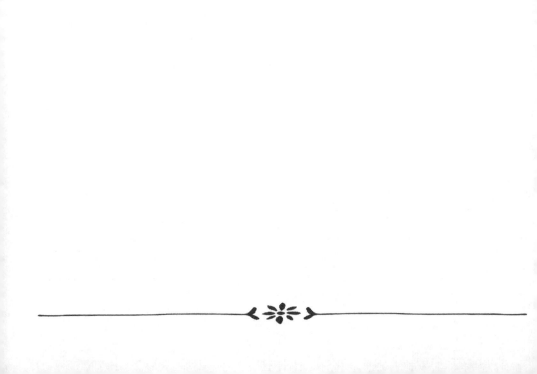

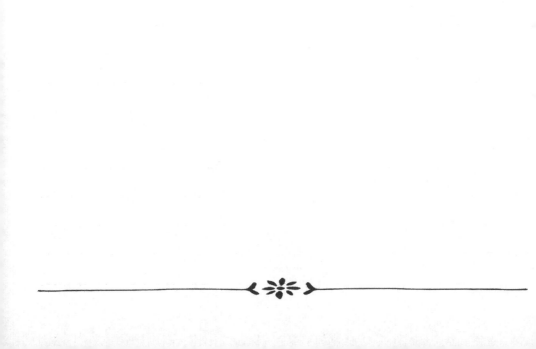

No act of kindness, no matter how small, is
ever wasted.

- Aesop

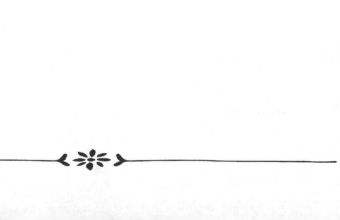

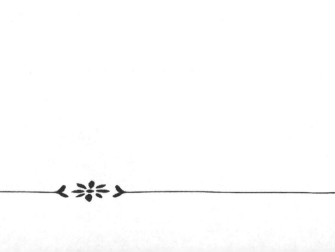

The way to be happy is to make others so.

– Robert Ingersoll

She is clothed in strength and
dignity and she laughs without fear
of the future.

— Proverbs 31:25 KJV

Peace is always beautiful.

– Walt Whitman

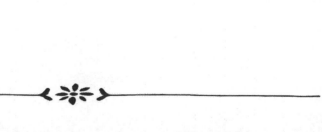

Don't hurry, be happy!

Bloom where you are planted.

- 1 Corinthians KJV